Lancashire C(
Including Pit Br(

on old picture po....

Norman Ellis

2. Men are pictured at the cage entrance of an Atherton Colliery. The mechanism allowed one cage to ascend as the other descended. The tracks facilitated the entry and removal of coal tubs. The Atherton Colliery Co produced a long series of postcards in the early 1900s to show aspects of pit life.

Picture postcards were first published in Britain in 1894, but it was not until a decade later that they began to take off, when in 1902 the Post Office allowed a message to be written on the address side. This meant that the whole of one side was available for the picture and obviously gave more scope to publishers. Photographic viewcards became very popular, and the postcard became the most important way of communicating news or messages, in much the same way as the telephone is used today. The years up to 1914 were the 'Golden Age' of picture postcards, when millions of imaginative designs covering every subject under the sun were published by a host of national and local firms. Today, these old postcards are keenly sought by historians and collectors.

Introduction

In 1891, a trainload of Wigan coalminers, returning from a trip to Southport, was held up at a signal box outside their home town. Across a flooded area, the colliers saw the elevated railway which linked Meadow Pit and Newtown Pit. In the dim light, the inebriated miners thought they were seeing Southport Pier again. Or had someone provided Wigan with a pleasure pier? Wigan in fact had several piers. They were stone and timber abutments, used as landing stages for coal on the Leeds & Liverpool Canal. The one which became known as Wigan Pier was Bankes Pier on the canal basin. It originated in the early 1820s and, via a tramway, provided a link to Stone House Colliery and later to other collieries. These were eventually acquired by Meyrick Bankes, who gave his name to the pier. This is the protuberance which appears on 'Wigan Pier' postcards.

Used for tipping coal into barges, the tippler mechanism on Wigan (Bankes) Pier was removed in 1929. The pier became a landing stage for passenger traffic. The area around the canal basin came to be known as Wigan Pier. The pier and basin were restored to remind visitors of the past importance of coal and the canal. Music hall jokes about the pier (and even Wigan itself) still occasionally surface.

To many people, Wigan presented the image of a typical northern industrial town – symbolic of dirt, squalor and misery. With springs of water containing medicinal properties, it might have become a spa in the eighteenth century, but the healing waters were drawn away by the sinking of coal pits. The coal was used to drive the cotton mills and provide warmth in the myriads of terraced houses. Ancillary to this was the working of iron ore, the production of steel and the making of machines. With excellent canal and rail facilities, some of the coal was despatched further afield. But the standard of housing and health, plus the high mortality rate, gave case for concern in Lancashire's coal capital, Wigan.

The workable Lancashire coalfield was confined to the south of the county, stretching from north of Burnley, down the western side of the Pennines to south of Manchester (into Cheshire) and westwards towards Liverpool. Several large and medium sized towns were centred in colliery areas, but also relied heavily on other industries, especially textiles, for their prosperity. The output of Lancashire coal peaked in 1907 at 26,000,000 tons from 358 pits; thereafter the production steadily declined, partly because of increasing difficulties in extracting coal from deeper seams. Heat and dust created conditions which were some of the worst anywhere. In neighbouring Yorkshire, in1907 and later, pits were still being sunk, and the future was bright enough to warrant the building of fine new colliery villages. In 1947, at Nationalisation, 74 Lancashire collieries were taken over by the National Coal Board, with a few remaining in private ownership.

In Victorian and Edwardian Wigan, around one in every five inhabitants was a Roman Catholic, partly a consequence of Irish immigration. The public houses offered colliers a chance to slake their thirst or get blind drunk. Colliery managers dreaded the resultant absenteeism. The churches and chapels persuaded people to 'sign the pledge'. They organised 'walking days' when banners were held high, and 'field days' with tea and sports. Varied entertainment was provided by the Royal Court Theatre and Grand Hippodrome; sport by the rugby league and swimming clubs. For enlightenment and education, there was Wigan Public Library and Wigan & District Mining & Technical College.

Female labour played a big part in some of the Lancashire collieries (notably at Wigan and Atherton), so a section of this book is devoted to these ladies. Apart from three cards kindly loaned to me by John Ryan, all the postcards (and a few cabinet prints) are from my collection, ploddingly put together over many years.

Norman Ellis, October 2012

ATHERTON COLLIERIES   PIT HEAD-GEAR.

3. Six miles east of Wigan is the smaller town of Atherton, whose growth, like Wigan's, was based on coal, cotton and iron. Eminent among its coal producers was Fletcher, Burrows & Co Ltd, owners of the four Atherton Collieries. Here, some modern metal lattice headgear is shown. This employer pursued an enlightened policy towards its employees. The company built good houses for its workers and provided facilities such as club houses, sports fields and bowling greens. Joint committees, chosen from the ranks of management and employees, were responsible for welfare matters. Pit head baths were opened as early as 1914.

Front Cover: Wigan photographer Thomas Taylor snapped a set of colliery scenes which appeared as colour tinted postcards in the 'Starr's CBB Series, Wigan', c.1910. Some of them are outdoor shots whilst others are below ground. Against a backdrop of headgear, screen buildings and pit props, this postcard shows colliers leaving work carrying their water or tea cans.

Back Cover (top): Pit brow girls, although not exclusive to Lancashire, were certainly a subject for many picture postcards produced in the county, particularly around Wigan and Atherton. Animated on-site examples eventually replaced studio portraits, such as these postcards in the Will Smith of Wigan Series.

Back Cover (bottom): The Tyldesley Coal Co Ltd worked several collieries in the Atherton area. It decorated this rulley with some of its products. Behind the display are two colliery-owned wagons and some fine colliery architecture.

4. Market Street, Atherton, is featured, c.1910, on a card published by Cartwright & Hall of 16 Market Street. Decorative tram standards hang over the single track. The splendid tower of the nineteenth century Church of St John the Baptist rises in the background.

5. Mineral extracted from a coal seam contained a percentage of dirt and stone. The grading and preparation for market was done at screening and washing plants, such as this at an Atherton Colliery. A shunting engine and two colliery-owned wagons are also featured.

6. The surface endless rope haulage installation shows full tubs on the left   and empty ones on the right, each with a clip for attaching to the rope. The system worked efficiently, except in atrocious weather. Several Atherton Colliery wagons stand in the yard.

7. In the tippler area of an Atherton Colliery, coal is being tipped from tubs to screens below. The reverse of the card carries a price list for various coals, including Arley large nuts (washed) at 10d per cwt. It was posted from a Fletcher, Burrows agent to Park House Hotel, Bolton, on 20 November 1906, perhaps as a reminder to stock up for winter.

8. This Atherton Colliery steam winding engine was made by Fraser & Chalmers of Erith. The clanging of signal bells was precursor to it starting up. In motion, it operated the cages in the pit shafts. It is obvious that parts of the engine were burnished until they shone.

9. Pewfall Colliery at Ashton-in-Markerfield was owned by Richard Evans & Co from 1860. It closed in 1911. On this card, posted from Haydock to Tranmere, Cheshire, in 1909, coal chutes are seen emanating from buildings in the left distance. The engine house in the foreground has interesting architecture.

10. By the 1930s, due to limited coal resources, most of the collieries in and around Skelmersdale had closed. White Moss Colliery was one of the last to go. Here, the exterior shots are complemented by men charging Lancashire boilers to raise steam for winding engines. The card, posted in 1925, was published by J W Hutchinson, pharmacist, Skelmersdale.

BLACUEGATE COLLIERY, SKELMERSDALE 26

11. Blacuegate Colliery at Skelmersdale was an early casualty, redundant miners being transferred to other pits further afield. Some of the laden wagons carry the name of the colliery. After the 1939-45 War, Skelmersdale was designated as a 'new town'. This is another Hutchinson postcard.

12. Golborne Colliery, at the edge of Golborne village, was one of several mines operated by Richard Evans & Co in the Haydock area. The headgear, screens and coal wagons (carrying the name Haydock) seem dwarfed by the tall chimney in this early 1900s view.

13. St Helens was a pioneering pit town. Bold Colliery, on the town's southeastern flank, belonged to the Collins Green Colliery Co and dated from 1875. A programme of deep boring by the National Coal Board in the 1950s led to reconstruction of its old buildings, seen here on a card posted in 1908.

14. Jubilee Colliery was at Crompton, near Shaw, a few miles southeast of Rochdale. Having been screen processed, coal from small corves is being lowered into a rail wagon via a chute. The railway line in the foreground carried it to the station yard at Shaw, there to be picked up by coal merchants.

15. The several small collieries in and around Cliviger village, near Burnley, belonged to the Cliviger Coal & Coke Co. Villagers are captured on camera, c.1905, in front of Copy Pit, Cliviger. In the middle 1930s, the colliery employed about forty people underground and eight above.

16. This and the next three pictures show aspects of underground work. They are from colour tinted photographs taken by Thomas Taylor and issued as postcards c.1910 in the 'Starr's CBB Series, Wigan'. The surveyor in the centre, probably testing for gas, is flanked by two younger men, scantily clad because of the heat.

17. Many severe and fatal accidents were caused by roof falls. These men, standing amidst timber pit props, are testing the roof. The large drill was used to make shot-firing holes. The original photographs, from which these postcards were issued, probably date from the turn of the century.

Junction in a coal mine.

18. Pit ponies performed all kinds of duties below ground, including shorter haulage journeys. These two probably had names and would be fed on hay and oats, plus tit-bits brought by miners. They were brought to the surface for a break during annual pit holidays.

Coal Mine-Haulage by endless rope.

19. The system of haulage by endless rope became popular below and above ground. The double-track mechanised haulage incorporated filled tubs going in one direction and empties going the other way. Belt conveyors eventually took over.

20. On postcards, there are several variations of the Lancashire Coat of Arms. Here, artist Jack Broadrick introduced a coal mining theme with a collier and his wife. The card was published by Dennis & Sons of Scarborough in their 'Dainty' series.

21. At the rear are checkweighmen, who monitored the weight of coal sent to the surface by each man. A management representative double checked this. The Thomas Taylor photograph was published in the 'Starr's CBB Series, Wigan'. It probably shows Moss Colliery at Ince. The pit brow girls are featured later in the book.

22. The Market Place at Wigan, coal capital of Lancashire, looks remarkably tidy. There are underground conveniences on the left. At right, between Wallaces and Craddocks, is the King's Head, one time meeting place of the Wigan Master Cloggers' Association. The Valentine's XL Series postcard was published by Bardale & Co, Blackburn.

23. The famous Wigan Pier on the Leeds & Liverpool Canal is shown, including the mechanism for tippling coal into barges (right of centre). This was removed in 1929, after coal transit declined. The pier became a starting point for trips. The canal basin and surrounding buildings now form a heritage centre.

24. The Wigan Coal & Iron Co Ltd owned numerous collieries. Because there were no iron ore reserves in the Wigan area, these were imported by canal and railway. The contents of the card, from Millard & Co, photographers, Market Street, Wigan, suggest that prosperity and pollution ran hand in hand.

25. Wigan Coal & Iron Co Ltd processed coal at its Semet Solvay plant to produce coke and other by-products. Distillation of the coal at high temperatures in the ovens was followed by discharge of red hot coke down the ramps, left. This is another Millard & Co postcard, c.1905.

26. This card was published by the Wigan Coal & Iron Co Ltd for the 1908 Franco-British Exhibition. The coal sections of this company became the Wigan Coal Corporation Ltd in 1930. At the same time, the iron and steel interests were absorbed by the Lancashire Steel Corporation.

27. The pits of Cross, Tetley & Co were located at Bamfurlong, three miles south of Wigan. Rail wagons and timber (for pit props) are visible beside the screening plant, left. The company became part of Wigan Coal Corporation in 1930.

28. Although Rochdale was not a colliery centre, its many mills and houses needed the fuel. It was delivered to sidings in the town by the Lancashire & Yorkshire Railway, to be moved on by coal merchants. Entwisle Road forms a backdrop for this tipping cart belonging to Laneside Coal Co.

29. Haydock, near St Helens, is famous for its racecourse, but the horse shown here is pulling a cart usually reserved for sacks of coal. The rail wagons in the background belonged to Haydock Coal Co, which had a prize band, consisting mainly of colliers.

30. The prestige of the Tyldesley Coal Co was raised when this decorated float paraded in the Tyldesley and Atherton areas. The dray carries a huge piece of coal and a model of pit headgear. Bricks and earthenware products are visible, made from clay often found near coal seams.

Coal Shute Worsley.

31. The third Duke of Bridgewater was responsible for building the Bridgewater Canal. Completed in 1761, it linked his colliery at Worsley to Manchester, eight miles away – and halved the price of coal there. This is the chute at Worsley where rail wagons tipped coal into barges.

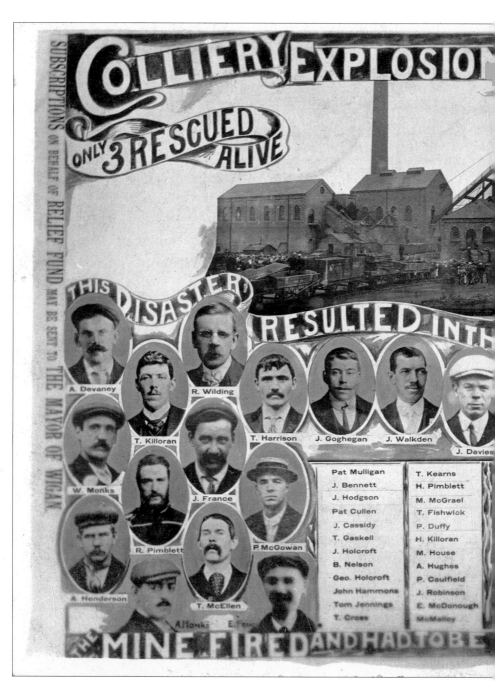

32. Maypole Colliery at Abram, near Wigan, was owned by Moss Hall Coal Co, later bec
of 18 August 1908, just after five, was caused by an underground explosion. At the tim
to the surface. The above postcard, published by Warner Gothard of Barnsley, indicat
rescued alive. The rescue party, working in appalling conditions, included a large conti

THE MAYPOLE PIT

ABRAM NR WIGAN

AUG 18TH 1908.

LOSS OF 76 LIVES

PUBLISHED BY W. GOTHARD, 6, ELDON STREET, BARNSLEY.

COPYRIGHT REGD.

J. Donlon
T. Donlon
Robinson
C. Ford
J. Kirby
G. Allen
J. Danson
A. Draper
J. Pennington
G. Melling
E Banks
P. Simm
J. Conway
P. Charnock

Sloyan | J. Moran
urns | M. Gallagher
. Grath | Thomas Groark
rehen | M. Cafferty
oyle | E. Cafferty
Boyle | T. M. Donald
vans | J. Flannery
urphy | McGuckien
Taylor | W. McCabe
Rushton | J. Taylor
loyd | J. Welsh
Carroll | W. Moore

OODED AFTER 7 WE RE BROUGHT TO THE SURFACE

g part of the Wigan Coal Corporation. The terrible disaster at Maypole on the afternoon
maintenance men and shot firers were in the pit, the day shift recently having returned
t 76 men lost their lives and lists 77. The true death toll was 75, with three men being
from Yorkshire.

ABRAM PIT DISASTER
AUG. 18. 1908.

33. Huge crowds soon gathered at Maypole Colliery on 18 August to await news about husbands, sons and fathers. This postcard, showing No.1 headgear, was probably issued a day or so after, and likely shows displaced miners, with one on the right reading a newspaper report of the tragedy. The colliery was still being developed at the time of the explosion, and was eventually reopened. Coal production finally ceased in 1934.

34. Beside the No.1 headgear of Maypole Colliery, extensive damage to the fan house on the left is visible, its roof having been blown off and lying at an angle. The huge fans had supplied air to the Maypole, and also supplemented supplies to nearby Junction Colliery.

THE ONLY SURVIVORS OF THE DISASTER AT THE MAYPOLE COLLIERY, ABRAM, AUGUST 18TH, 1908.

Will Smith Series, Wigan. Copyright.

EDWARD FARRELL, 3, CAMBRIDGE ST., WIGAN.   WM. DORAN, 5, HARDYBUTTS, WIGAN.   RICHARD FAIRHURST, 11, CROWN STREET, HINDLEY.

35. Edward Farrell, William Doran and Richard Fairhurst were the sole survivors of the disaster at Maypole Colliery. They had been working in a different part of the mine to the men who perished. The postcard was published in the Will Smith series.

HULTON COLLIERY DISASTER.

R. Byers.

TOMB OF THE 24 UNIDENTIFIED BODIES, WESTHOUGHTON CEMETERY.

P. Westhead (since dec'd),   G. Gleaves,   A. Nuttall,
Chairman,   Ex-Chairman,   Cemetery Chairman.
              Westhoughton District Council.

36. The worst colliery disaster in Lancashire was the explosion of firedamp and coal dust at the Hulton Colliery Company's Pretoria Pit (near Bolton) on 21 December 1910, when 344 men and boys lost their lives. The grave of 24 unidentified bodies at Westhoughton is pictured. Various burial grounds were used for the other victims.

37. This fully-kitted mine rescue team was attached to Pemberton Colliery at Leigh. Larger collieries had one or more rescue brigades; smaller pits called on the services of a central rescue station. The postcard was published by F Devereux of the Royal Photo Co at Leigh.

38. On 28 June 1927, the Prince of Wales visited Blackpool to open the new Miners' Convalescent Home. The card was published by the Scholastic Souvenir Co of Bispham and posted from the home on 8 November 1927 to a Mrs Cook at St Helens. 'From home to home' according to the message.

39. The reading room at he Miners' Convalescent Home, Blackpool, was well equipped with books, newspapers and seating - to provide for the inner man as well as his physical needs. The stylish home cost £160,000 to build and equip. It had beds for 132 men. The card was produced by SS Photos of Blackpool, c.1930.

Pit Brow Girls

The use of female labour down the pits goes back as far as the collieries themselves; well before the days when coal production was managed by large companies, some of which owned several collieries. Many of the early mines were bell pits or 'day holes' operated by a family or group of families. Mothers, boys and girls were expected to contribute to the coal getting. Being part of the family, the children had some protection. Male colliers sometimes paid people to work for them. Women working in underground areas moved coal by carrying, dragging on sledges or pushing or pulling in trolleys. Contemporary drawings show women crawling along the floor, harnessed by a belt or rope around the shoulders and waist and a chain passing between their legs and hooked to a tub. Boys and girls helped with this work, as well as performing other duties, such as raising coal to the surface with a windlass.

According to the 1841 census, there were 118,233 coal miners in Britain, of whom 2,350 were women. Around one third of these females worked in Lancashire. Following a government investigation in 1842, it became illegal to employ boys under the age of ten and all girls and women underground. For a time, some women continued to be employed illegally underground. Ultimately, the act was enforced, but not without objections from the women themselves. Around Wigan, some of the females moved to the mills. Others obtained jobs at the pit top – either sorting coal at the screens or manoeuvring tubs.

Prior to the advent of screening plant, coal was given some hand riddling underground or at the surface before it was shovelled into wagons. In many areas, including Lancashire, the work became the prerogative of females, known as 'pit brow girls'. By the1870s, screens were being developed which separated the coal into different sizes. The early screens consisted of wooden bars on a sloping plain, set at a fixed distance apart. Vibrating screens were later introduced (called 'shakers' in Lancashire).

Tipplers dropped coal on to the screens, via a chute with a trapdoor at the bottom to regulate the flow. The coal was transferred to moving belts at the foot of the screens. Pit brow women were employed on the tipplers, screens and especially the belts. There they manually checked the coal and removed 'dirt'. They used long-handled rakes to obviate blockages. Large lumps of coal were removed for breaking with a hammer. As demand for different sizes and types of coal increased, the screen and belt arrangements became more versatile. Coal was a wasteful product, as became evident by the many slag heaps which appeared.

Picture postcards and 'cabinet' prints are the best illustrated sources for any study of pit brow girls, but must be scrutinized with caution, especially those which are studio portraits. Both the photographer and the photographed may have been more concerned to produce an attractive image rather than an authentic one. Was there a specious hint of glamour in some of the portraits? The workaday attire of pit brow girls drew criticism from do-gooders, who claimed that shawls or long skirts might become caught in machinery. A converse idea was that trousers were for men only. Cambridge academic Arthur Joseph Munby (1828-1910) produced diaries which provide some insight into the life of the women. In the Wigan area, the pit brow girls feature on postcards by Will Smith, Thomas Taylor and Herbert Wragg, The early work of the latter appeared on cabinet prints from c.1885.

Although picture postcards were first published in Britain in 1894, it was 1902 when the Post Office permitted the message to be written on the address side, thus allowing the whole of the other side to be used for the picture. By 1904, good photographic postcards were becoming popular. Herbert Wragg turned his attention to them, probably utilizing the same negatives used for his cabinet prints.

40. National postcard publisher Valentines of Dundee produced this view of the pit head at Strangeways Hall Colliery, near Wigan, c.1905. The pit was owned by Crompton & Shawcross Ltd. Unusually, the card is captioned 'work girls'. They are featured in workaday clothes, the younger ones crouched at the front.

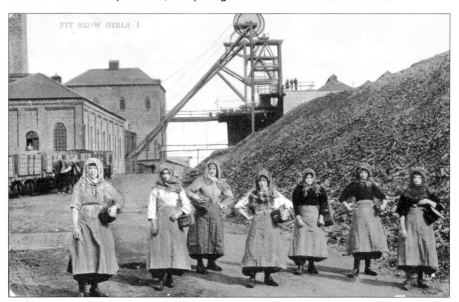

41. This view shows a 'magnificent seven' pit brow girls in front of Junction Colliery, near Wigan. All of them are carrying snap baskets. Sunk in 1887, the colliery finally closed in 1962. This and the next four postcards form part of the 'Will Smith's Series, Wigan' dating from c.1905.

42. Pit brow girls manoeuvre tubs at the Arley Mine of the Moss Hall Coal Co, Ince, near Wigan A double-type hoist, for raising tubs from below, is visible in the background, right.

43. Four pit brow girls, using rakes, are screening coal dropped from a tippler above on to an inclined chute which has bars. Part way up is a plate for controlling the flow. The girls are wearing old jackets to keep warm.

44. These pit brow girls have posed beside some pit tubs. Two of the lasses are wielding small hammers, used for splitting or chipping larger lumps of coal on the screening belts. In the background, right, is a tub hoist.

45. Another group of pit brow girls barely managed to say 'cheese' to the camera. This and the four previous postcards are based on hand coloured photographs. Whilst the colours may be subject to some artistic license, the actual clothing is probably authentic. This contrasts somewhat with the more presentable attire on some of the studio portraits which follow.

46. This cabinet print probably dates from c.1890. Its outside measurements are 6½" x 4¼" (against 5½" x 3½" for a postcard). It was produced by Herbert Wragg, artist & photographer, in his studio at 45 Mesnes Street, Wigan. The original photo, stuck on to the thick card, is a rich chocolate/sepia colour. The young pit brow girl is Ann Holland, aged 16. She appears against a studio backcloth holding a typical colliery shovel and riddle. Her dress might be described as a glamorized version of that worn at the pit brow.

47. Set against the same studio background, but with additional props, is another pit brow lady, Mrs Roscoe, aged 37. This cabinet also was produced by Herbert Wragg. The tidy apparel must only be regarded as symbolic of actual clothing worn at the pit. Possibly it was the property of the studio. Note the high polish on the clasp-fastening clogs.

48. The third cabinet from the Wragg studio portrays an attractive pit brow girl whose name and age are not known. The two shovels are those appearing in the previous views, and the clothing looks very similar. All three cabinets are the same size and have identical backs. The negatives probably were kept and used later to produce postcards.

49. The same Wragg background appears again, this time on a postcard, but the workaday garb of the girls is in sharp contrast to that on the previous portraits. The postcard was issued c.1905, but the photograph may be earlier.

Could you but see my Nancy, among the tubs of coal,
In tucked up skirt and breeches, she looks exceeding droll,
Her face besmeared with coal dust, as black as black can be,
She is a pit brow lassie, but she's all the world to me.   Anon.

50. In front of the familiar Wragg background is a trio of pit brow girls on a postcard from c.1905. They are in working day clothing, holding lunch baskets and tea or water cans. Perhaps this is a family group, with the three ladies being spouses of colliers.

51. Posted from Wigan to Southport in 1904, the message on this card reads, "*These creatures are more plentiful here than in Southport. Please do not mistake them for lady motor cyclists, because they are not*". The famous postcard publisher Wrench issued this studio portrait.

Colliery Girls.

LANCASHIRE PIT BROW GIRLS

Taylor's Series.   IN PIT ATTIRE AND ORDINARY DRESS.   *Copyright.*

52. Thomas Taylor of Platt Bridge, Wigan, produced this postcard of pit brow girls in colliery attire and Sunday best. The first picture has a pit brow location; the other a studio background.

53. This fine postcard of pit brow girls in the Wigan area was produced by Wragg, c.1905, although the actual photograph may have been taken up to a a decade earlier. Wearing chic shawls, the ladies are arranged at the pit head of their unidentified colliery.

54. This and the next three postcards feature pit brow girls at Douglas Bank Colliery to the west of Wigan, c.1905. Here, at the enclosed pit brow, the hoist in the centre was used for raising or lowering tubs. The card was published by Millard & Co, photographers, 70 Market Street, Wigan. James Millard and his son William were keen local photographers.

55. Eight pit brow girls are pictured doing various jobs at the screening plant of Douglas Bank Colliery (named after the River Douglas). They probably lived in nearby terrace houses on Holt Street or Canal Street. Although not credited, this card likely came from the Millard studio.

56. A pit brow girl has temporarily discarded her shovel and taken centre stage in the screening area of Douglas Bank Colliery. The pit was noted for its high quality 'cannel' coal, which produced few ashes and little smoke. The postcard is credited to the Millard & Co studio.

57. A number of conveyor belts and a skip are shown at Douglas Bank Colliery, where pit brow girls used eyes and hands to check coal and remove dirt. The colliery closed down in 1921. Although not stated, this must be another Millard postcard.

58. Smiles and laughter permeate this parade of pit brow girls at Gibfield Colliery, Atherton, one of the pits owned by Fletcher, Burrows & Co Ltd. The pit became part of Manchester Collieries Ltd and lasted until 1963, by then in National Coal Board ownership.

59. Pit brow girls are pictured beside shaker screens at Chanters Colliery, another Fletcher, Burrows colliery at Atherton. The lady on the left is lowering her pick to chip a large lump of coal. In 1938, the pit, by then under Manchester Collieries ownership, still employed about 1,200 people. It closed in 1966.